CHILDREN'S Jazz Chants

OLD AND NEW

CAROLYN GRAHAM

OXFORD
UNIVERSITY PRESS

OXFORD
UNIVERSITY PRESS

198 Madison Avenue
New York, NY 10016 USA

Great Clarendon Street
Oxford OX2 6DP England

Oxford New York

Auckland Bangkok Buenos Aires Cape Town Chennai Dar es Salaam Delhi
Hong Kong Istanbul Karachi Kolkata Kuala Lumpur Madrid Melbourne
Mexico City Mumbai Nairobi São Paulo Shanghai Singapore Taipei Tokyo Toronto

with an associated company in *Berlin*

OXFORD is a trademark of Oxford University Press.

ISBN 0-19-433721-9

Copyright © 2002 Oxford University Press

Editorial Manager: Nancy Leonhardt
Senior Production Editor: Joseph McGasko
Art Director: Lynn Luchetti
Senior Designer: Maj-Britt Hagsted
Production Manager: Shanta Persaud
Production Coordinator: Eve Wong

Developmental Editor: Marilyn Rosenthal
Editorial, Design, and Production Services: BookLinks Publishing Services

Illustrations by Joy Allen, Nan Brooks, Gwen Connelly, Kate Flannigan, Ruth Flannigan, Angela Kamstra, Valerie Sokolova, Kristina Stephenson, Rebecca Thornburg, Lucia Washburn

"A Bird Has Wings," "Mosquitos Bite," and "My Favorite Color is Yellow" are reprinted with permission of Delta Systems Co., Inc.

Cover Design by BookLinks Publishing Services / Maj-Britt Hagsted
Cover Calligraphy by Don Grimes

Cover Illustrations by Ruth Flannigan and Valerie Sokolova

Printing (last digit): 10 9 8 7 6 5 4 3 2 1

Printed in Hong Kong.

Acknowledgments

Dr. Marilyn Rosenthal, Developmental Editor, deserves very special recognition, for without her, *Jazz Chants* would not have happened. She was the original editor of the first edition of *Jazz Chants* and has been a valued and important part of the *Jazz Chants* series since the beginning. She has once more put her enormous talent and energy into making this book the very best it can be. I value her not only as a trusted colleague, but as a dear and faithful friend.

I would like to thank June Schwartz, Editorial Project Manager, for her very helpful and tireless efforts to make this book a reality. Her musical talent was a wonderful help in the direction of the recording sessions, and her marvelous attention to detail helped shape the look of the book as well as the sound of the recording.

I would like to express my appreciation to Joey Mennonna for his brilliant work in arranging and performing the music on the accompanying cassette and CD.

Very special thanks to Sally Woodson, who brought her special talent to the recording studio, and to the children who sang and chanted under her splendid direction. Thanks also to all of the people at Full House Productions for their patience and skill during the recording.

And finally, I would like to thank the designers at OUP and BookLinks, and the managers of OUP, for their wonderful support of this project.

Carolyn Graham

This book is dedicated to my friend Marina Boquet in Dijon with affection and admiration for her wonderful performance of "The Yellow Chair Chant" in Amiens.

Table of Contents

Part 3: New Chants

Part 4: New Songs

Part 5: Teacher's Notes for Chants and Songs

Structure Key

Structure	Chant or Song	Page

Structure	Chant or Song	Page

Structure	Chant or Song	Page

Introduction

What Is a Jazz Chant®?

Jazz Chants® are the rhythmic expression of standard American English. Just as the selection of a particular tempo and beat in jazz may convey powerful and varied emotions, the rhythm, stress, and intonation patterns of spoken language are essential elements for the expression of feelings and intent of the speaker. By setting our natural language to rhythm and/or music, Carolyn Graham created the concept of Jazz Chants® as a powerful language teaching technique, especially for young children.

The original *Jazz Chants® for Children* was first published in 1979 by Oxford University Press, and the use of these chants and songs to teach English has spread as a phenomenon throughout the world. Jazz Chants are particularly unique in that they emphasize the natural rhythm of conversational English and never distort the language. The strong rhythmic patterns of the chants and songs bear a close relationship to children's games, and to children's natural affinity for rhythm and movement.

What Is *Children's Jazz Chants® Old and New* ?

Children's Jazz Chants® Old and New by Carolyn Graham is a collection of 50 chants and songs. Twenty-five of these are chants and songs from Carolyn Graham's classic *Jazz Chants® for Children*. Twenty five are new chants and songs.

The book is divided into 5 parts.

Part 1: Classic Chants (15 of the best loved chants from the original book)

Part 2: Classic Songs (10 of the best loved songs from the original book)

Part 3: New Chants (10 new chants)

Part 4: New Songs (15 new songs)

Part 5: Specific Teacher's Notes for each of the above sections. These notes highlight the specific structures, pronunciation, and vocabulary for each chant and song in the book. In addition, there are special performance suggestions as appropriate.

The chants and songs presented in this book focus on natural language: on vocabulary, expressions, and structures used by children in everyday situations. Many of the chants involve student interaction and movement. Colorful illustrations reinforce the meaning of the targeted language by depicting the situations and vocabulary of the chant or song. Musical notation is provided for each song. A Structure Key on pages vi–ix lists the chants and songs by the various structures found in each.

Children's Jazz Chants® Old and New Cassette/Compact Disc

All of the chants and songs are featured on the recording, available on cassette or compact disc (CD). The chants and songs from the original *Jazz Chants® for Children* have been rerecorded using new musical arrangements. The recording, which uses children's voices, is useful for providing the underlying rhythm of the chants and songs, and for providing a model for students to follow.

Suggestions for Presenting the Chants and Songs

Step 1

Preview the name of the chant or song and its vocabulary, using the illustrations to support your instruction whenever possible.

Step 2

Play the recording once or twice to allow students to become familiar with the words and rhythm of the chant or the melody of the song. Some of the song melodies are traditional ones that students may know. Encourage students to tap out the rhythm or move to the beat as they listen to the chant or song.

Step 3

Teach the chant or song line-by-line. With their books still closed, students should repeat each line after you. Or, use the recording to model each line. Some teachers teach the song as a chant first, and then present it with the melody.

Note: The symbol that appears in some of the chant lines (*) represents claps. These claps are part of the rhythm of the chant and can be helpful to the oral performance of the chants.

Step 4

Have students open their books. Play the recording again. Have students read along with the text, silently at first, so that they can begin associating the rhythm and intonation of the chant or song with the words printed on the page. Play the recording again. This time, have students chant or sing along with the recording (as a whole class).

Step 5

Once students are comfortable with the song or chant, create various performance arrangements for them. For example, if a chant is interactive (has questions and answers, like a dialogue), divide the class into two groups and have each group take the role of a speaker. Here is an example using the chant *I Found a Cow*:

> Group 1: I found a cow!
>
> Group 2: How?
>
> Group 1: I found a bear!
>
> Group 2: Where?

Some chants work especially well when the students perform them with a chorus and individual solos. Here is an example using the chant *Three Black Sheep*:

> Solo 1: Three black sheep fast asleep.
>
> Chorus: Three black sheep fast asleep.
>
> Solo 2: Spiders in the sun having fun.
>
> Chorus: Three black sheep fast asleep.

For chants or songs that are divided into two or more verses, you can assign a verse to each group, and have students stand when it is their turn to perform. There are many possibilities; allow your students to help you create interesting arrangements for the chants and songs, including combinations of solos, pairs, and small groups.

Some chants and songs lend themselves well to gestures or mime. Lead your students with gestures whenever possible, as it will make the experience more natural and fun, especially for younger or more shy students. Also, encourage students to bring in percussion instruments (particularly ones from their own cultures) such as tambourines, maracas, or bells.

Extending and Reinforcing the Language in the Chants and Songs

There are many activities you can do to extend and reinforce the language presented in the chants and songs. A few examples follow.

Personalize the Chants and Songs

Students enjoy chants and songs even more when they have created them themselves. Whenever possible, substitute students' real information in the song or chant. For example, in the chant *Who Is Sylvia?*, in the line *Who has a name that starts with S?*, substitute children's real names that start with S.

> Group: Who has a name that starts with **S**?
>
> Student 1: I do.
>
> Group: She does.
>
> Student 2: What's her name?
>
> Group: Sari.

You could also have students substitute a different initial letter using real students' names. For example:

> Group: Who has a name that starts with **J**?
>
> Student 1: I do.
>
> Group: He does.
>
> Student 2: What's his name?
>
> Group: Juan.

When students create their own chants and songs, don't insist that all the lines rhyme. Rhymes do make the chant or song easier to memorize, but they can sometimes be more difficult to create.

"Cloze" the Chants and Songs

A "cloze" activity is one in which students have to fill in blanks or come up with a missing word or phrase. This activity can be done orally or in writing. One way to do it is to chant or sing part of a line, then stop, and have students chant or sing the remainder of the phrase. Here is an example using the chant *Wonderful Dream*:

> Teacher: I had a dream last night...
> Students: ...a wonderful dream.

Another way to do a "cloze" activity is to replace a word in the middle of a sentence or phrase with a clap, and elicit that word from the students. For example:

> Teacher: Soup in a (clap), peanut butter (clap), and a gingerbread (clap)
> Students: can...cookies...man

"Chunk" the Language of the Chants and Songs

A language "chunk" is a word or phrase that is isolated from a larger segment. Select certain vocabulary, idioms, or phrases from the body of the chant or song and create new arrangements to practice the language. Here is an example using selected language chunks from *The Toothbrush Song:*

Group 1: Toothbrush, toothbrush, toothbrush, toothbrush

Group 2: Hairbrush, hairbrush, hairbrush, hairbrush

Group 3: Washcloth, washcloth, washcloth, washcloth

Have the three groups take turns chanting their parts. If desired, have each group chant their lines louder and louder each time. As a variation, have the three groups alternate their lines:

Group 1: Toothbrush

Group 2: Hairbrush

Group 3: Washcloth

Group 1: Toothbrush

Group 2: Hairbrush

Group 3: Washcloth

Role Play and Movement with the Chants and Songs

Many learners can retain new language better when they associate it with movement. Certain chants and songs will lend themselves well to activities involving movement. The class can do the movements together, or you can assign roles to particular students, who will then dramatize these roles while the rest of the class is chanting or singing. Using the chant *A Bird Has Wings* as an example, have various students role-play being the different animals. Select one student to be a bird and flap his or her wings as the class chants *A bird has wings, two wings.* Select two other students to act out flapping their wings as the class chants *Two little birds, four little wings.*

Select one student to be a dog and wag his or her imaginary tail as the class chants *One little dog, one little tail.* Two other students wag their tails as the class chants *Two little dogs, two little tails.*

You can continue this and have students create their own movements and chants. For example, if four "little bird" students come to the front of the room and flap their wings, the class would then have to appropriately chant *Four little birds, eight little wings.* Another example of this type of activity would be for students to pantomime the various actions in the song *I Feel Terrible* as the class is singing the song. For example, *I've got a headache, I've got a toothache,* etc.

Have Students Share Their Cultures

Encourage students to share various related themes, customs, or types of language (greetings, words for different animal sounds, etc.) from their own cultures. For example, in the song *Giraffes Drink Water,* if students live in a culture where there are real giraffes, encourage them to talk about this. Another example would be to have students sing *The Hot Dog Song* and then make up a song about food in their culture(s). Or, have students give the equivalent in their language of a cat saying "Meow" in English. Encourage students when possible to bring in their own musical instruments from their culture and to generate their own chants or songs based on the themes in this book.

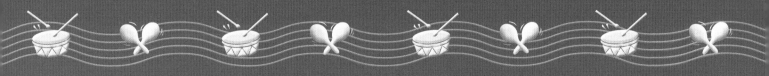

Part 1:
Classic Chants

Shoes and Socks

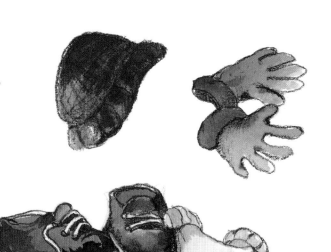

What do you wear on your head?
   A hat.
What do you wear on your hands?
   Gloves.
What do you wear on your feet?
   Socks.
   Shoes and socks.
   Shoes and socks.

What do you wear when it's cold?
   Socks.
   Shoes and socks.
   Shoes and socks.

What do you wear when it's warm?
   Socks.
   Shoes and socks.
   Shoes and socks.

Where do you wear your hat?
   On my head.
Where do you wear your gloves?
   On my hands.
What do you wear on your feet?
   Socks.
   Shoes and socks.
   Shoes and socks.

Who Is Sylvia?

Who has a name that starts with **S**?
 I do.
  She does.
What's her name?
  Sylvia!

Who has a name that ends with **A**?
 I do.
  She does.
What's her name?
  Sylvia!

Who has a name with a **V** in the middle?
 I do.
  She does.
What's her name?
  Sylvia!

Who has a name with an **L** in the middle?
 I do.
  She does.
What's her name?
  Sylvia!

Who is Sylvia?
 I am.
  She is.
What's her name?

Mosquitos Bite

Mosquitos bite.
Bees sting.
Cats sleep.
Birds sing.

Bunnies hop.
Tigers fight.
Turtles swim.
Sharks bite.

Frogs jump
all around.
Bats hang
upside down.

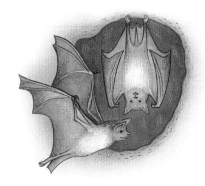

Where's Jack?

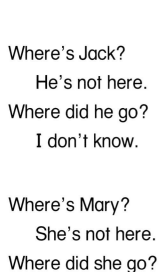

Where's Jack?
    He's not here.
Where did he go?
    I don't know.

Where's Mary?
    She's not here.
Where did she go?
    I don't know.

Where are Sue and Bobby?
    They're not here.
Where did they go?
    I don't know.

Where's Mr. Brown?
    He's over there.
Where?
    Over there,
    asleep in the chair.

You Did It Again!

You did it again!
    What did I do?
You did it again!
    What did I do?
I told you not to do it,
and you did it again!
    I'm sorry. I'm sorry.

You broke it!
    What did I break?
You took it!
    What did I take?
You lost it!
    What did I lose?
You chose it!
    What did I choose?
I told you not to do it,
and you did it again!
    I'm sorry. I'm sorry.

You wore it!
    What did I wear?
You tore it!
    What did I tear?
I told you not to do it,
and you did it again!
    I'm sorry. I'm sorry.

🦅 A Bird Has Wings

A bird has wings, two wings.
One little bird.
    Two little wings.
Two little birds.
    Four little wings.
A bird has wings, two wings.

A dog has a tail, one tail.
One little dog.
    One little tail.
Two little dogs.
    Two little tails.
A dog has a tail, one tail.

A cat has ears, two ears.
One little cat.
    Two little ears.
Two little cats.
    Four little ears.
A cat has ears, two ears.

Three big, blue birds.
    Six big, blue wings.
Four big, brown dogs.
    Four big, brown tails.

Stop That Noise!

Sh! Sh! Stop that noise!
　Sh! Sh! Stop that noise!

Come on girls. Come on boys.
Tell everybody to stop that noise!

　Please be quiet! Stop that noise!
　Please be quiet! Stop that noise!
　Please be quiet! Stop that noise!

Tell everybody to stop that noise!

　Keep it down! Stop that noise!
　Keep it down! Stop that noise!
　Keep it down! Stop that noise!

Tell everybody to stop that noise!

　Sh! Sh! Stop that noise!
　Sh! Sh! Stop that noise!
　Sh! Sh! Stop that noise!

Tell everybody to stop that noise!

Scaredy Cat

I'm afraid of the dark.
   Don't be silly.
I'm afraid of the dark.
   Don't be silly.
I'm scared of the dark.
   Don't be silly.
   Don't be silly.
I'm afraid of the dark.

Turn on the lights!
   Don't be silly.
Turn on the lights!
   Don't be silly.
Turn on the lights!
   Don't be silly.

Turn them on!
   Turn them off!
Turn them on!
   Turn them off!
Turn them on!
   Don't be silly.
   Don't be silly.
I'm afraid of the dark.

I'm scared of the dark.
   She's scared of the dark.
   Scaredy cat! Scaredy cat!
I'm scared of the dark.
   She's scared of the dark.
   Scaredy cat! Scaredy cat!

Turn on the lights!
   Don't be silly.
   Scaredy cat!
I'm afraid of the dark.

I Asked My Father

I asked my father.
  What did he say?
Papa said, "No, no, no."
I asked my mother.
  What did she say?
Mama said, "Yes, yes, yes."

I asked my father for a dollar and a half.
  What did he say?
"No, no."
I asked my mother for fifty cents.
  What did she say?
"No, no."

I asked Mom again.
  What did she say?
My mother said, "Ask your father."
I asked Dad again.
  What did he say?
My father said, "Ask your mother."

I asked my mother for a candy bar.
  What did she say?
"No, no."
I asked my father for some lemonade.
  What did he say?
"Yes, yes."

I Found a Cow

I found a cow!
How?
I found a cow!
How?

I found a bear!
Where?
I found a bear!
Where?

I found a hen!
When?
I found a hen!
When?

I found a cow.
I found a bear.
I found a hen.
When?

I found a hen.
I found a cow.
I found a bear.
Where?

I found a bear.
I found a hen.
I found a cow.
How?

I found a bear.
I found a hen.
I found a cow.
Wow!

Mama! Mama! My Socks Don't Match!

Mama! Mama! My socks don't match!
One is red and one is blue.
One is bigger than the other!
    Oh, no!

    Mama! Mama! My socks don't match!
    One is bigger than the other!
        Oh, no!

Mama! Mama! My shoes don't match!
One is black and one is brown.
One is bigger than the other!
    Oh, no!

    Mama! Mama! My feet don't match.
    One is bigger than the other!
        Oh, no!

I Like My Friends

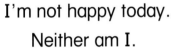

I like my friends.
   So do I.
I like my old friends.
   So do I.
I like my new friends.
   So do I.
I'm happy today.
   So am I.

I don't like my friends.
   Neither do I.
I don't like my old friends.
   Neither do I.
I don't like my new friends.
   Neither do I.
I'm not happy today.
   Neither am I.

I don't like my socks.
   I don't either.
I don't like my books.
   I don't either.
I don't like my shoes.
   I don't either.
I'm not happy today.
   I'm not either.

I like my clothes.
   I do, too.
I like my old clothes.
   I do, too.
I like my new clothes.
   I do, too.
I'm happy today
   I am, too.

Grandma's Going to the Grocery Store

Grandma's going to the grocery store.
    One, two, three, four.
Grandma's going to the grocery store.
    One, two, three, four.

Who's going?
    Grandma's going.
Who's going?
    Grandma's going.
Where's she going?
    To the grocery store.
    One, two, three, four.

When's she going?
    At a quarter after four.
    One, two, three, four.
What's she going to buy at the grocery store?
    One, two, three, four.
What's she going to buy at the grocery store?
    One, two, three, four.

A loaf of bread,
a bottle of milk,
a big bag of cookies,
and a little can of peas.

A loaf of bread,
a bottle of milk,
a big bag of cookies,
and a little can of peas.

Grandma's going to the grocery store.
One, two, three, four.
Grandma's going to the grocery store.
One, two, three, four.

Polka Dot Pajamas

I woke up early.
    Early in the morning
Got out of bed.
    Comfortable bed.
Jumped on the pillow.
    Soft pillow.
Stood on my head.
    Hard head.

Took off my pajamas.
    Polka dot pajamas.
Put on my clothes.
    Beautiful clothes.
Brushed my teeth.
    Nice white teeth.
Blew my nose.
    Tiny little nose.
Had my breakfast.
    Great big breakfast.
Fed the cat.
    Fat cat.

Went back to my room.
  Nice little room.
Opened the door.
  Great big door.
Saw my pajamas.
  Polka dot pajamas.
On the floor.
  Polka dot pajamas.
Picked them up.
  Polka dot pajamas.
Put them in a drawer.
  Polka dot pajamas.

Picked up my books.
  Three or four.
Said goodbye to Mama,
and ran out the door.

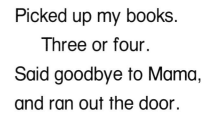

I Bought a Dog for My Cat

I bought a dog for my cat.
  The cat didn't like the dog. Meow!

I bought a bird for my cat.
  The cat didn't like the bird. Meow!

I bought a house for the dog.
  The dog didn't like the house. Grrr!

I bought a cage for the bird.
  The bird didn't like the cage. Peep!

The cat didn't like the dog. Meow!
The dog didn't like the cat. Grrr!
Nobody liked the bird. Peep!
Nobody liked the bird. Peep!

Part 2:
Classic Songs

Ernie

The Hot Dog Song

Melody: Have You Ever Seen a Lassie?

Have you ev - er had a hot dog with mus - tard and

mayon-naise? Have you ev - er had a hot dog with pep - per and

salt? With mus - tard and mayon-naise and ketch - up and

pickl - es. Have you ev - er had a hot dog with pep - per and

salt? With mus - tard and mayon-naise, and let - tuce and

on - ions, and mus - tard and mayon-naise, and ketch - up and

pick - les, and mus - tard and mayon-naise, and let - tuce and

on - ions, and mus-tard and mayon-naise, and pep - per and salt.

22

The Sun Is Shining

The sun is shin - ing.___ I love the sun. Me, too.

The sun is shin - ing. I love the sun. Me, too. The sun is shin - ing.___

I love the sun. The sun is shin-ing to - day. It's

rain - ing to - day.___ I love the rain. Not me. It's
snow - ing to - day.___ I love the snow. I'm cold. It's

rain - ing to - day.___ I love the rain. Not me. It's rain - ing to - day.___
snow-ing to - day.___ I love the snow. I'm cold. It's snow-ing to - day.___

I love the rain. It's rain - ing, rain-ing to - day. It's
I love the snow. It's snow - ing, snow-ing to - day.

Downtown

Melody: The Peacherine Rag

24

♪♫ The Elbows Song

Melody: Will the Circle Be Unbroken?

Take your el - bows off the ta - ble. Keep those big feet on the floor. Take your hat off when you come in. You're not out - side an - y - more.

Keep your mouth shut when you're eat - ing.

If you're hun - gry, ask for more.

But take your el - bows off the ta - ble,

and keep those big feet on the floor.

♪♪ My Favorite Color Is Yellow

Melody: My Bonnie Lies Over the Ocean

♪♫ I Feel Terrible

Melody: La Cucaracha

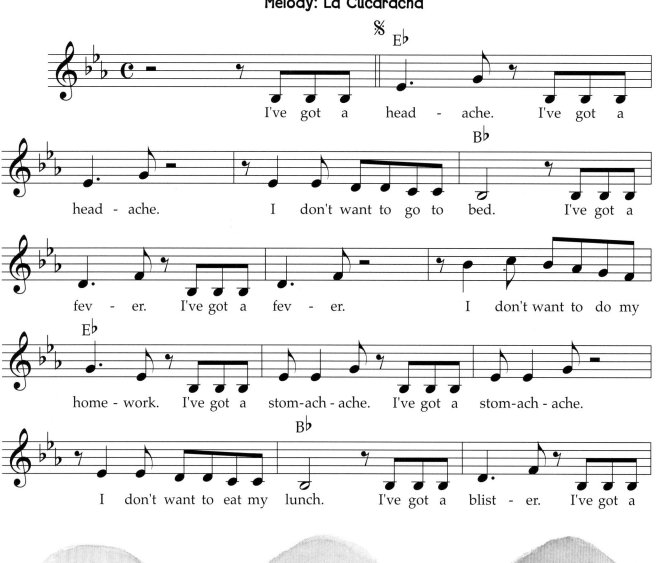

I've got a head - ache. I've got a
head - ache. I don't want to go to bed. I've got a
fev - er. I've got a fev - er. I don't want to do my
home - work. I've got a stom-ach - ache. I've got a stom-ach - ache.
I don't want to eat my lunch. I've got a blist - er. I've got a

blist - er. I don't want to see my sist - er. *Fine*

Ever - y time I get a head - ache.___ Ma - ma takes me to the
Ever - y time I get a tooth - ache.___ Ma - ma takes me to the

doc - tor.___ Ever - y time I get a fev - er.___
dent - ist.___ Ever - y time I see the den - tist.___

Ma - ma takes me to the nurse.
I al - ways come home feel - ing worse.

I've got a
D.S. al Fine

♪♫ The Shoulder Song

F
One head, two should-ers. Two eyes, two should-ers.
Two arms, two el - bows. Two arms, two el - bows.

C   F   C
One mouth, two should-ers. How man-y toes? Ten toes.____
Two legs, two ank - les. How man-y toes? Ten toes.____

F
One head, two should-ers. One nose, two should-ers.
Two hands, ten fing - ers. Two hands, ten fing - ers.

B♭   F   C   F
Two arms,____ two____ should - ers. How man-y toes? Ten toes.
Two ank - les, two____ el - bows. How man-y toes? Ten toes.

♪♫ Monkeys Swing

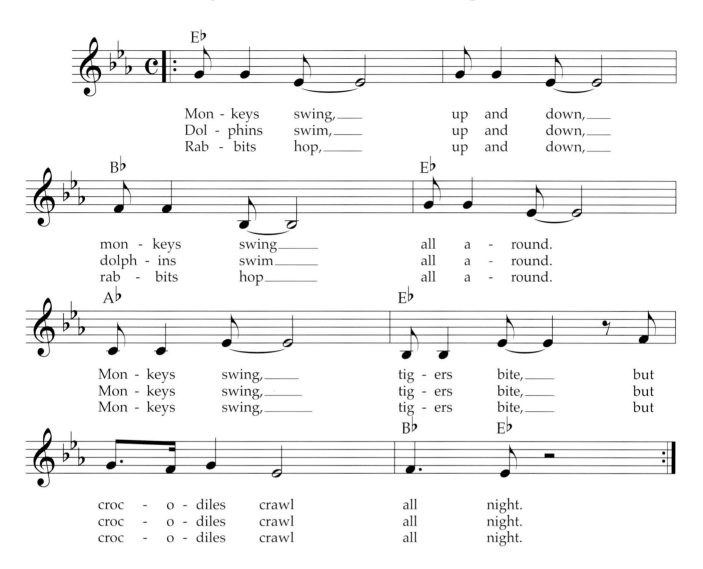

Mon - keys swing,____ up and down,____
Dol - phins swim,____ up and down,____
Rab - bits hop,____ up and down,____

mon - keys swing____ all a - round.
dolph - ins swim____ all a - round.
rab - bits hop____ all a - round.

Mon - keys swing,____ tig - ers bite,____ but
Mon - keys swing,____ tig - ers bite,____ but
Mon - keys swing,____ tig - ers bite,____ but

croc - o - diles crawl all night.
croc - o - diles crawl all night.
croc - o - diles crawl all night.

The Horse March

Melody: Stars and Stripes Forever

I wish I had a horse. I wish I had a horse of my own. And if I had a horse of my own, that horse would nev-er be lone - ly. If I had a horse of my own, he would stay ev-er-y day by my win - dow. If I had a horse of my own, he would nev-er___ be a-lone. If I had a horse of my own, he would stay ev-er-y day right by my win - dow. If I had a horse of my own, I on-ly know that horse and I would not be lone - ly.

34

Part 3:
New Chants

Three Black Sheep

Three black sheep
fast asleep.

> Three black sheep
> fast asleep.

Spiders in the sun
having fun.

> Three black sheep
> fast asleep.

Puppies in a box
eating socks.

> Three black sheep
> fast asleep.

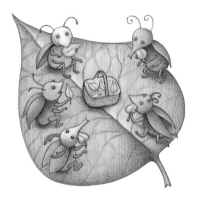

Beetles in a bunch
having lunch.

> Three black sheep
> fast asleep.

Skunks in glasses
going to their classes.

> Three black sheep
> fast asleep.

Three black sheep
fast asleep.

> Three black sheep
> fast asleep.

Fleas Love Dogs

Fleas love dogs.
Rats love cheese.
Fleas love dogs,
but dogs hate fleas.

Fleas love cats.
Rats love cheese.
Fleas love cats,
but cats hate fleas.

Dogs hate cats.
Cats hate fleas.
Fleas like dogs and cats and cheese.

Do you like dogs?
 Yes, I do.
Do you like cheese?
 Yes, I do.
Do you like cats?
 Yes, I do.
 I do, too.
 I do, too.

I love dogs and cats and cheese,
but I don't like rats and I don't like fleas.

I'm Thinking of a Word

I'm thinking of a word that starts with **P**.

    How many letters?

One, two, three.

It starts with **P** and ends with **G.**

    I know the answer:

    P - I - G!

I'm thinking of a word that starts with **C**.

    How many letters?

One, two, three.

It starts with **C** and ends with **T.**

    I know the answer:

    C - A - T!

I'm thinking of a word that starts with **D**.

    How many letters?

One, two, three.

It starts with **D** and ends with **G.**

    I know the answer:

    D - O - G!

Wonderful Dream

I had a dream last night,
a wonderful dream.

I had a dream last night,
a wonderful dream.

What did you dream about?

Soup in a can,
peanut butter cookies,
and a gingerbread man.

Chocolate candy,
a strawberry shake,
birthday candles on a birthday cake.

I had a dream last night,
a wonderful dream.

I had a dream last night,
a wonderful dream.

What did you dream about?

Soup in a can,
peanut butter cookies,
and a gingerbread man.

The Dinosaur Chant

I saw a dinosaur.

What did you see?

I saw a dinosaur swinging from a tree.

I met a dinosaur waiting for a train.

I saw a dinosaur dancing in the rain.

I found a dinosaur sitting in the park.

I heard a dinosaur singing in the dark.

I heard a dinosaur say, "Hello."

I heard a dinosaur say, "Let's go!"

I smiled at him and said, "O.K."

He said, "See you later, alligator.

Have a nice day."

Because I Forgot to Wake Up the Cow

Because I forgot to wake up the cow,
the cow forgot to wake up the cat,
the cat forgot to wake up the dog,
so we all missed lunch.

Because I forgot to go to the store,
the dog forgot to shut the door,
the door forgot to wake up the floor,
so we all missed lunch.

Because I forgot to tell the bird,
the bird forgot to tell the dog,
the dog forgot to tell the cow,
so we all missed lunch.

The Backpack Chant

Backpack, backpack.
What's in your backpack?
What's in your backpack?

Lots of things:
textbooks, notebooks,
paper clips, thumbtacks,
pens, pencils,
keys on a ring.

Backpack, backpack.
What's in your backpack?
What's in your backpack?

Lots of things:
a calculator,
candy bars,
scissors, string.

What's in your backpack?
Everything!

Early Bird

I'm an early bird.
I love to get up
very early in the morning.

She's an early bird.
She loves to get up
very early in the morning.

I'm a night owl.
I hate to get up
very early in the morning.

He's a night owl.
He hates to get up
very early in the morning.

I'm an early bird.
I love the sun.

She's an early bird.
She loves the sun.

I'm a night owl.
I love the moon.

He's a night owl.
He loves the moon.

She loves to get up.
He hates to get up
very early in the morning.

The Homework Chant

Homework, homework.
Lots of homework.
Early in the morning.
Late at night.

Mary does homework.
Mary loves homework.
      Mary *loves* homework?
* That's right!

Homework, homework.
Lots of homework.
Early in the morning.
Late at night.

Harry does homework.
Harry hates homework.
      Harry *hates* homework?
* That's right!

The Broccoli Chant

I hate broccoli.
   So do I.
   I really don't like it.
   I don't know why.

I can't stand it.
What can I say?
I hope we don't have it for lunch today!

I love broccoli.
   So do I.
   I really like it.
   I don't know why.

I'm crazy about it.
What can I say?
I hope we have it for lunch today!

Part 4:
New Songs

The Sad Dog Song

Hel - lo, good dog.____ You look sad.

What's the mat - ter?____ I feel bad.

Good dog,____ good dog.____ What can I do?

What's the prob - lem? I feel blue. Good dog, good dog.____

Don't feel bad. What's the mat - ter?____ I feel sad.

Good dog,____ tell me,____ please. What's wrong?

48

The Four Seasons Song

The Happy Kangaroo Song

How are you, kan-ga-roo? How are you? Kan-gar-oo, kan-ga-roo. How are you? I'm a hap-py kan-ga-roo. How are you? How are you? I'm hap-py, too, kan-ga-roo.

Where's Diana?

Where's Di - a - na? Where's Di - a - na? D - I - A - N - A.

Where's Di - a - na? I want to see Di - a - na ever - y day. Where is she? Where's Ro - ber - to?

Where's Ro - ber - to? R - O - B - E - R - T - O.____

Where's Ro - ber - to? I want to see Ro - ber - to ever - y day.

Giraffes Drink Water

Gir - affes drink wat - er.___ Gir - affes eat leaves. Gir -

affes al - most nev - er, nev - er, nev - er eat cheese! They

don't like beet - les.___ Gir - affes hate bees.

When they're ver - y hun - gry,___ gir - affes eat trees!

The Toothbrush Song

C

Tooth - brush,   tooth - brush.   Brush   your   teeth   with   a
Hair - brush,   hair - brush.   Brush   your   hair   with   a
Wash - cloth,   wash - cloth.   Wash   your   face   with   a
Tooth - brush,   tooth - brush.   Brush   your   teeth   with   a

G   **C**

tooth-brush, tooth-brush.   Brush your teeth with a   tooth - brush,   tooth - brush.
hair - brush, hair - brush.   Brush you hair with a   hair - brush,   hair - brush.
wash - cloth, wash - cloth.   Wash your face with a   wash - cloth,   wash - cloth.
tooth-brush, tooth-brush.   Brush your teeth with a   tooth - brush,   tooth - brush.

F   **C**   **G**   **C**

Brush   your   teeth.   Comb   your   hair   with   a   comb.
Brush   your   hair.   Comb   your   hair   with   a   comb.
Wash   your   face.   Dry   your   face   with   a   towel.
Brush   your   teeth.   Comb   your   hair   with   a   comb.

♪♫ T—Telephone

C

T— Tel - e - phone   V— Vid - e - o
C— Cell - u - lar   T— Tel - e - phone
T— Tel - e - phone   V— Vid - e - o

C   **F**

T— Tel - e - phone   V— Vid - e - o
C— Cell - ul - ar   T— Tel - e - phone
T— Tel - e - phone   V— Vid - e - o

C   **G7**

T— Tel - e - phone   V— Vid - e - o
C— Cell - u - lar   T— Tel - e - phone
T— Tel - e - phone   V— Vid - e - o

C   **G**   **C**   **G7**

T - V   T - V
Cell phone   Cell phone.   Hello?
T - V   T - V   *Fine*

55

He's an Ethiopian

Back in School

🎵 The Good Student Song

Melody: The Old Gray Mare

He gets up earl-y and * goes to En-glish class, * goes to En-glish class, * goes to En-glish class. He gets up earl-y and * goes to En-glish class. He's nev-er, ev-er late to school. Nev-er, ev-er late to school. Nev-er, ev-er late to school. He gets up earl-y and * goes to En-glish class. He's nev-er, ev-er late to school. She comes home earl-y and * does her home-work, * does her home-work, * does her home-work. She comes home earl-y and

* does her home-work. She's nev-er, ev-er late to school.

Nev-er, ev-er late to school. Nev-er, ev-er late to

school. She comes home earl-y and * does her home-work. She's

nev-er, ev-er late to school.

♪♫ Danny Bought a D-O-G

Dan - ny bought a D - O - G.
Dan - ny lost his D - O - G.
Dan - ny found his D - O - G.

Dan - ny bought a D - O - G.
Dan - ny lost his D - O - G.
Dan - ny found his D - O - G.

Dan - ny bought a D - O - G. Oh___ gee oh!___
Dan - ny lost his D - O - G. Oh___ gee oh!___
Dan - ny found his D - O - G. Oh___ gee oh!___

Dan - ny bought a D - O - G.
Dan - ny lost his D - O - G.
Dan - ny found his D - O - G.

♪♫ Hi, How Are You?

G

Hi, how are you? I'm fine, thank you._____

C

Hi, how are you? I'm fine, thank you._____

D   **G**   **D**   **G**

Hi, how are you? I'm fine, how are you? I'm fine, thank___you. I'm fine.

The Happy Weekend Song

Melody: Skip To My Lou

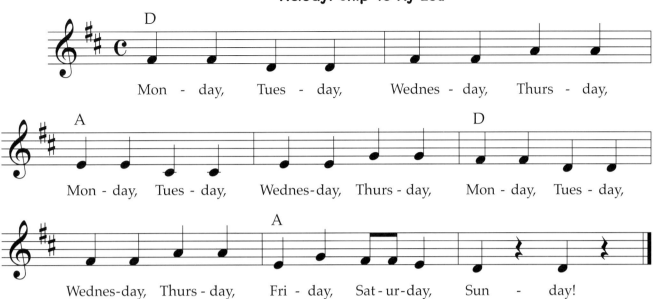

D

Mon - day, Tues - day, Wednes - day, Thurs - day,

A   D

Mon - day, Tues - day, Wednes-day, Thurs-day, Mon - day, Tues - day,

A

Wednes-day, Thurs - day, Fri - day, Sat - ur-day, Sun - day!

I Bought a House for My Pig

I bought a house for my pig. I
put my pig on the floor. I fed my pig, but he
got so big, he could-n't get out of the door. He got
big - ger and big - ger and big - ger and big - ger and WOW!
Look at him now! I bought a house for my

cat.   I   put   my   cat   on   the   floor.   I

fed   my cat, but she   got   so fat,   she could-n't get out of the

door.   She got   big-ger and big-ger and big-ger and big-ger and

WOW!   Look at her   now!

♪♫ If It Rains

If it rains, I'll wear my rain-coat. If it
rains, we'll wear our rain-coats. If it

does-n't rain, I won't. When it's cold, I al-ways
does-n't rain, we won't. When it's cold, we al-ways

wear my gloves. When it is-n't cold, I don't. If it
wear our gloves. When it is-n't cold, we don't. If it

snows, I won't wear san-dals. If the sun comes out, I
snows, we won't wear san-dals. If the sun comes out, we

will. If it rains, I'll wear my brand new coat. If I
will. If it rains, we'll wear our brand new coats. If we

don't, I'll get a chill. If it
don't, we'll get get a chill. *Fine*

Part 5:
Teacher's Notes
Chants and Songs

Shoes and Socks (Page 2)

STRUCTURES
- Simple present information questions with *what/where: What do you wear on…?, What do you wear when…?, Where do you wear your…?*
- Indefinite article a: *a hat*
- Possessive adjectives: *your, my*
- Regular noun plurals: *gloves, shoes, socks*
- Irregular noun plurals: *feet*

PRONUNCIATION
- *S* sound of the plural *s: socks*
- *Z* sound of the plural *s: gloves, shoes*
- The reduction of *and* to *'n: shoes 'n socks*
- Contractions: *it's*
- Note that *wear* and *where* sound alike.

VOCABULARY
- Parts of the body: *head, hands, feet*
- Clothing: *hat, gloves, shoes, socks*

Who Is Sylvia? (Page 3)

STRUCTURES
- Simple present information questions with *who/what: Who has a name that starts…, Who has a name with a…, Who is Sylvia?, What's her name?*
- Short answers: *I do., She does., I am., She is.*
- Simple present, third person *s: starts, ends*
- Irregular verbs: *have, be, do*
- Indefinite article *a, an: a V, an L*
- Prepositional phrases: *in the middle*
- Possessive adjectives: *her*

PRONUNCIATION
- Contractions: *what's*
- Disappearing *h* when it occurs in *What's her name? (What's 'er)*
- *Th* sound in *with*
- *S* sound of third person *s: starts*
- *Z* sound of third person *s: ends*
- The sounds of the letters of the alphabet (S,Y,L,V,I,A)

VOCABULARY
- The names of the letters of the alphabet (S,Y,L,V,I,A)

PERFORMANCE NOTES
- Practice this chant with three groups or solo voices.
- Substitute other students' names after the class has practiced with "Sylvia."
- Have students shout out the names of the letters *S, Y, L, V, I, A.*

Mosquitos Bite (Page 4)

STRUCTURES
- Simple present statements: *Mosquitos bite, Bees sting,* etc.
- Regular noun plurals: *mosquitos, bees, cats, birds, bunnies, tigers, turtles, sharks, frogs, bats*

PRONUNCIATION
- *Z* sound of the plural *s: mosquitos, bees, bunnies, birds, tigers, turtles, frogs*
- *S* sound of the plural *s: cats, sharks, bats*
- Rhyming patterns: *sting/sing, bite/fight, all around/upside down*

VOCABULARY
- Action words: *bite, sting, sleep, sing, hop, fight, swim, jump, hang upside down*

PERFORMANCE NOTES
- Have students pantomime the action words: *bite, sting, sleep, sing, hop, swim, fight, jump, hang upside down*

Where's Jack? (Page 5)

STRUCTURES
- Simple present information questions with *where: Where's Jack?, Where are Sue and Bobby?*
- Simple past information questions with *where: Where did he go?, Where did they go?*
- Subject pronouns: *he, she, I, they*
- Subject pronouns contracted with verb BE: *he's, she's, they're*
- Negative statements: *He's not here., I don't know.*
- Prepositional phrases: *in the chair*

PRONUNCIATION
- Contractions: *where's, he's, she's, they're*
- Rhyming patterns: *go/know, there/chair*

You Did It Again (Page 6)

STRUCTURES
- Simple past statements: *You did it again!, I told you not to do it..., You broke it!,* etc.
- Simple past irregular verbs: *do/did, break/broke, take/took, lose/lost, choose/chose, wear/wore, tear/tore*
- Simple past information questions with *what: What did I do?, What did I break?,* etc.

PRONUNCIATION
- Contractions: *I'm*
- Rhyming patterns: *break/take, lose/choose, wear/tear*

VOCABULARY
- The language of apology: *I'm sorry.*

A Bird Has Wings (Page 7)

STRUCTURES
- Simple present statements: *A bird has wings..., A dog has a tail..., A cat has ears...*
- *Have* as a main verb.
- Indefinite article *a: a bird, a tail*
- Absence of the article in the plural statement: *A cat has ears.*
- Adjective order: Number + Size + Color + Noun: *three big, blue birds*

PRONUNCIATION
- *Z* sound of the plural *s: wings, tails, ears, birds, dogs*

VOCABULARY
- Colors: *blue, brown*
- *Bird, dog, cat, wings, tails, ears*

PERFORMANCE NOTES
- Have students pantomime the number of birds and the number of their wings.
- Have students pantomime the number of cats and dogs and the number of their ears and tails.

Stop That Noise! (Page 8)

STRUCTURES
- Simple present commands: *Stop that noise!, Tell everybody*
- Regular noun plurals: *boys, girls*

PRONUNCIATION
- Rhyming pattern: *noise/boys*
- *Z* sound of the plural *s: boys, girls*

VOCABULARY
- Polite requests: *Please*
- Commands: *Keep it down!, stop, tell*
- *Everybody, girls, boys*

Scaredy Cat (Page 9)

STRUCTURES
- Simple present commands: *Don't be silly., Turn on the lights!, Turn them on!, Turn them off!*

PRONUNCIATION
- Contractions: *I'm*

VOCABULARY
- Language to express fear: *I'm afraid., I'm scared.*
- Language to reassure: *Don't be silly.*
- *Scaredy cat*: Childhood expression for someone who is easily frightened.

Teacher's Notes Classic Chants

I Asked My Father (Page 10)

STRUCTURES
- Simple past statements: *I asked my father., I asked my mother.*, etc.
- Simple past information questions with *what: What did he say?, What did she say?*
- Possessive adjectives: *my, your*
- Subject pronouns: *he, she*
- Indefinite article: *a dollar and a half, a candy bar*

PRONUNCIATION
- *T* sound of the past tense verb ending in *asked*
- Reduction of the *h* sound in *he: What did he say?*
- Reduction of the word and to *'n: a dollar 'n a half*
- *S* sound of the plural *s: cents*

VOCABULARY
- *Mom, Dad, father, mother*
- *A dollar and a half, fifty cents, candy bar, lemonade, some*

I Found a Cow (Page 11)

STRUCTURES
- Simple past statements: *I found a (cow)!*
- Irregular past verb form: *find/found*
- Question words: *how, where, when*
- Indefinite article *a: a cow*

PRONUNCIATION
- Falling intonation pattern on the question words, *how, where, when*
- Rhyming patterns: *cow/how, bear/where, hen/when, cow/wow*

VOCABULARY
- *Cow, bear, when*
- Exclamation: *Wow!*

Mama! Mama! My Socks Don't Match! (Page 12)

STRUCTURES
- Simple present negative statements: *My (socks) don't match!*
- Comparative adjectives: *bigger*
- Regular plural nouns: *socks, shoes*
- Irregular plural nouns: *feet*
- Possessive adjectives: *my*

PRONUNCIATION
- *S* sound of the plural *s: socks*
- *Z* sound of the plural *s: shoes*
- *Ch* sound in *match*
- Falling/rising/falling intonation pattern of *Oh, no!*

VOCABULARY
- Colors: *red, blue, black, brown*
- Expression of sympathy: *Oh, no!*

I Like My Friends (Page 13)

STRUCTURES
- Simple present affirmative and negative statements: *I like my (friends). I don't like my (friends).*
- Verbs: *like, be, do*
- Contractions: *I'm*
- Affirmative short response: *So am I., I am, too., So do I., I do, too.*
- Negative short response: *I don't either., Neither do I.*

PRONUNCIATION
- *Z* sound of the plural *s: friends, shoes, clothes*
- *S* sound of the plural *s: socks, books*

VOCABULARY
- *Books, clothes, friends, shoes, socks, new, old, happy, today*

Grandma's Going to the Grocery Store (Page 14)

STRUCTURES
- Present continuous statements: *Grandma's going to the grocery store.*
- Simple present information questions with *who/where/when/what: Who's going?, Where's she going?, When's she going?, What's she going to buy...?*
- Indefinite article *a: a loaf of bread, a bottle of milk, a big bag of cookies, a little can of peas*
- Prepositional phrases: *at the grocery store, at a quarter after four, to the grocery store*

PRONUNCIATION
- Contractions: *who's, where's, when's, what's, Grandma's*
- Reduction of the *-ing* sound to the sound *-in' (goin')* in *Grandma's going to the grocery store,* but not in sentence final position, *Grandma's going.*
- Reduction of the words *going to* to *gonna* in *What's she going to buy,* but not in *Grandma's going to the grocery store.*
- Rising intonation for clarification in *Who's going?*
- Rising/falling intonation in other information questions: *Where's she going?, What's she going to buy at the grocery store?*

VOCABULARY
- Quantifiers: *a loaf of, a bottle of, a bag of, a can of*
- Grocery items: *bread, milk, cookies, peas*
- Numbers 1–4
- Adjectives: *big, little*

PERFORMANCE NOTES
- Have students take turns pantomiming the role of Grandma.

Polka Dot Pajamas (Page 16)

STRUCTURES
- Simple past affirmative statements: *I woke up early. Got out of bed.,* etc.
- Simple past regular and irregular verbs: *woke up, got out of, jumped on, stood on, took off, put on, brushed, blew, had, fed, went back, opened, saw, picked up, said, ran*
- Adjective + noun: *comfortable bed, soft pillow, hard head, beautiful clothes, nice white teeth, tiny little nose, nice little room, polka dot pajamas*
- Two-word verbs: *took off, put on, picked up*
- Prepositional phrases: *on the floor, in a drawer, on my head, in the morning*

PRONUNCIATION
- *Z* sound of the plural s: *pajamas, clothes*
- *T* sound of the past tense ending: *jumped, brushed, picked up*
- *D* sound of the past tense ending: *opened*
- Reduction of *out of* to *outta.*

VOCABULARY
- Part of the body: *head, teeth, nose*
- *Bed, pillow, pajamas, room, door, drawer, books, breakfast*
- Time expression: *early in the morning*

I Bought a Dog for My Cat (Page 18)

STRUCTURES
- Simple past affirmative statements: *I bought a dog for my cat., I bought a bird for my cat., I bought a house for the dog., I bought a cage for the bird.*
- Simple past negative statements: *The cat didn't like the dog., The cat didn't like the bird., The dog didn't like the house., The bird didn't like the cage., The dog didn't like the cat., Nobody liked the bird.*

PRONUNCIATION
- The slightly exaggerated *ow* sound in *Meow* and the *ee* sound in *Peep*
- *T* sound of the past tense ending: *liked*

VOCABULARY
- Animals: *dog, cat, bird*
- *Cage, house*
- Words for animal sounds in English. Note that in different languages, there are different words for these same animal sounds.

PERFORMANCE NOTES
- Have students try to sound like the animals when they make the sounds *meow, grrr,* and *peep*.

Teacher's Notes Classic Songs

Ernie (Page 20)

STRUCTURES
- Simple present
- Information questions with *where*: *Where's Ernie?*
- Affirmative statements: *It's Ernie.*
- Negative statements: *I don't know.*

PRONUNCIATION
- Contractions: *where's, it's, don't*

VOCABULARY
- Greetings: *Good morning, Hello, Goodbye*

PERFORMANCE NOTES
- Have one student take the role of Ernie and do a little walk or a little dance across the classroom waving "hello, good morning," and "goodbye." He points to himself as students sing the chorus, *It's Ernie! Hello, Ernie.*
- Substitute students' real names for "Ernie" and have them take turns playing the role of Ernie.

The Hot Dog Song (Page 22)

STRUCTURES
- Present perfect questions: *Have you ever had...*

PRONUNCIATION
- Reduction in the sound of *and* to *'n* : *mustard and mayonnaise*
- *Z* sound of the plural *s* in pickles and onions
- *Th* sound in *with*
- The pronunciation of *ketchup* varies regionally and can be either *ketch-up, catch-up,* or *catsup.*

VOCABULARY
- Food items: *hot dog, lettuce*
- Condiments/seasonings: *mustard, mayonnaise, pepper, salt, onions, ketchup*

The Sun Is Shining (Page 23)

STRUCTURES
- Present continuous: *The sun is shining.*
- Simple present: *I love the sun.*
- Short phrases of agreement/disagreement: *Me, too./Not me.*

PRONUNCIATION
- Sound of the ending *-ing*: *shining, raining, snowing*
- Contractions: *it's, I'm*

VOCABULARY
- Weather words: *the sun, shining, the rain, raining, the snow, snowing, cold*

Downtown (Page 24)

STRUCTURES
- Simple present statements: *I want to go...*
- Future with *BE + going to: I'm going to ride...*
- Conditional: *If you want to...*
- Future with *will: We'll have a wonderful time.*
- Modal *can* for permission. *You can go with me...*

PRONUNCIATION
- Reduction of *want to* to *wanna: I want to go downtown., I want to fool around,* but not in *If you want to, you can go with me.*
- Reduction of *going to* to *gonna: I'm going to ride..., I'm going to jump..., I'm going to watch..., I'm going to say...*

VOCABULARY
- Nouns: *bike, school, swimming pool, people*
- Verbs: *go, ride, jump, watch, want, say*
- Expressions: *fool around* (have fun), *have a wonderful time, come and go*

The Elbows Song (Page 26)

STRUCTURES
- Simple present commands: *Take your elbows...,Keep those big feet...,Take your hat off...,Keep your mouth shut...*
- Adverbial clauses of time: *...when you come in., ...when you're eating.*
- Conditional: *If you're hungry...*
- Prepositional phrases: *on the floor*

PRONUNCIATION
- *Z* sound of the plural *s*: *elbows*
- Contractions: *you're*
- Note that the contraction *you're* and the possessive adjective *your* sound alike.

VOCABULARY
- Parts of the body: *elbows, feet, mouth*
- *table, floor, hat, outside, anymore*

My Favorite Color Is Yellow (Page 28)

STRUCTURES
- Simple present affirmative statements: *My favorite color is yellow, My favorite number...,* etc.
- Possessive adjectives: *my*
- Object pronouns: *you*

PRONUNCIATION
- Syllable reduction in *chocolate* to a two syllable word: *choc-late*
- Note the American English spelling of the word *color* instead of the British English word *colour*. The pronunciation is the same.

VOCABULARY
- *favorite, person, color, number, flavor, yellow, two, chocolate.*

PERFORMANCE NOTES:
- Have students join hands and form a circle. If possible, have them pass a (yellow) ribbon around the circle as they sing this song. When they get to the words *my favorite person is you*, the movement of the ribbon stops and students shout out the name of the person holding the ribbon. Then they use that student's name in place of the word Billy in the chorus. For

example, if the ribbon stops at Kenji, students shout *Kenji*. Then they sing *Kenji, Kenji, my favorite person is you, is you. Kenji, Kenji, my favorite person is you.*

I Feel Terrible (Page 30)

STRUCTURES
- Simple present affirmative statements: *I've got a headache.*
- Simple present negative statements: *I don't want to go to bed.*
- Indefinite article *a: a headache, a fever*
- Definite article *the: the nurse, the doctor*
- Possessive adjectives: *my*
- Irregular comparatives: *worse*

PRONUNCIATION
- Reduction of *got + a* to *gotta: I've got a headache., I've got a fever.*
- Reduction of *get + a* to *getta: Every time I get a toothache...*
- Reduction of *want to* to *wanna: I don't want to eat my lunch.*
- Rhyming patterns: *blister / sister, nurse / worse*

VOCABULARY
- Health vocabulary: *headache, stomachache, toothache, fever, blister, doctor, dentist, nurse*
- *bed, lunch, sister, Mama, every time*

Teacher's Notes Classic Songs

The Shoulder Song (Page 32)
STRUCTURES
- Information questions with *How many: How many toes?*
(Note ellipses of verb *BE* in this very conversational style as opposed to *How many toes are there?*)
- Singular / plural contrast: *one head, two shoulders*

PRONUNCIATION
- *Z* sound of the plural *s* in *shoulders, eyes, arms, elbows, legs, ankles, toes, hands, fingers*
- Rhyming patterns: *nose / toes*

VOCABULARY
- Parts of the body: *head, shoulders, eye, mouth, nose, arms, elbows, legs, ankles, hands, fingers, toes*

Monkeys Swing (Page 33)
STRUCTURES
- Simple present affirmative statements: *Monkeys swing..., tigers bite...,* etc.
- Compound sentences with but: *Monkeys swing, tigers bite, but crocodiles crawl all night.*

PRONUNCIATION
- *Z* sound of the plural *s: monkeys, tigers, crocodiles, dolphins*
- *S* sound of the plural *s: rabbits, elephants*

VOCABULARY
- Animal names: *monkeys, tigers, crocodiles, dolphins, rabbits, elephants.*
- Action verbs: *swing, bite, crawl, swim, hop.*

PERFORMANCE NOTES
- Have students pantomime the various actions of the animals (swing, bite, crawl, swim, hop). When they say *tigers bite*, they should overemphasize the ferocity of the word *bite*.

The Horse March (Page 34)
STRUCTURES
- Unreal conditional: *I wish I had..., If I had..., ...he would...*
- Indefinite article *a: a horse*
- Possessive adjectives: *my*

PRONUNCIATION
- Rhyming patterns: *own / alone, stay / day*

VOCABULARY
- *Horse, lonely, window, never, own, alone*
- Expressions: *right by* (directly next to), *I only know* (emphatic form for *I know one thing for sure*)

Teacher's Notes New Chants

Three Black Sheep (Page 37)

STRUCTURES
- Present continuous with *BE* omitted: *Spiders in the sun having fun, Puppies in a box eating socks.*
- Verbs forms: *having, eating, going*
- Regular plural nouns: *spiders, beetles, skunks, socks, classes, glasses, puppies*
- Irregular plural nouns: *sheep*
- Prepositional phrases: *in the sun, in a bunch, in a box*
- Possessive adjectives: *their*

PRONUNCIATION
- *Z* sound of the plural s: *beetles, spiders, puppies*
- *S* sound of the plural *s: skunks, socks*
- *Z* sound of the plural *s: glasses, classes*
- Final *ch* sound: *bunch, lunch*
- rhyming patterns: *sheep/asleep, sun/fun, box/socks, bunch/lunch, glasses/classes*

VOCABULARY
- Animal names: *sheep, spiders, puppies, beetles, skunks*
- Expressions: *fast asleep* (in a very deep sleep)

Fleas Love Dogs (Page 38)

STRUCTURES
- Simple present affirmative statements: *Fleas love dogs., Rats love cheese.*
- Simple present negative statements: *I don't like rats ...,I don't like fleas.*
- Compound sentences with *but: Fleas love cats, but cats hate fleas.*
- Compound sentences with *and: I don't like rats and I don't like fleas.*

PRONUNCIATION
- Reduction of *and* to *'n: dogs and cats*
- *Z* sound of the plural *s: fleas, dogs*
- *S* sound of the plural *s: rats, cats*
- Rhyming patterns: *cheese/fleas*

VOCABULARY
- Animal names: *fleas, dogs, rats, cats*
- Language for expressing likes and dislikes: *like, don't like, love, hate*

I'm Thinking of a Word (Page 39)

STRUCTURES
- Present Continuous: *I'm thinking of a word...*
- Simple present: *It starts with P and ends with G.*
- Relative clauses with *that: I'm thinking of a word that starts with P.*
- Simple present information questions with *How many: How many letters?*
- Prepositions: *with*
- Indefinite article *a: a word*
- Definite article *the: the answer*

PRONUNCIATION
- *S* sound of the third person simple present verb: *starts*
- *Z* sound of the third person simple present verb: *ends*
- The names of the letters of the alphabet: *P,I,G, C,A,T, D, O, G*
- Reduction of *and* to *'n: It starts with P and ends with G.*
- Rhyming patterns: *P/three/G, C/three/T, D/three/ G*

VOCABULARY
- The names of the letters of the alphabet: *P,I,G, C,A,T, D, O, G*
- Animal names: *pig, cat, dog*
- Numbers: *one, two, three*

Teacher's Notes New Chants

Wonderful Dream (Page 40)
STRUCTURES
- Simple past affirmative statements: *I had a dream last night...*
- Simple past information questions with *what: What did you dream about?*
- Indefinite article *a: a dream, a can, a birthday cake*

PRONUNCIATION
- *Z* sound of the plural *s: cookies*
- Rhyming patterns: *can/man, shake/cake*

VOCABULARY
- Food words: *soup, peanut butter cookies, chocolate candy, strawberry shake, birthday cake, gingerbread man*
- *Dream, birthday candles, can*

The Dinosaur Chant (Page 41)
STRUCTURES
- Simple past affirmative statements: *I saw a dinosaur.*
- Simple past information questions with *what: What did you see?*
- Direct address: *I heard a dinosaur say, "Hello.", I heard a dinosaur say, "Let's go!", I smiled at him and said, "O.K.", He said, "See you later, alligator. Have a nice day."*
- Indefinite article *a: a dinosaur*
- Prepositional phrases: *from a tree, in the rain, in the park, in the dark*

PRONUNCIATION
- Full, final *-ing* sound of the endings on : *swinging, waiting, dancing, singing.*
- rhyming patterns: *see/tree, train/rain, park/dark, hello/let's go, later/alligator, O.K./day*

VOCABULARY
- *Dinosaur, tree, train, park, dark, day, rain, hello, let's go*
- Expressions: *O.K., Have a nice day., See you later, alligator.* (humorous form for *Goodbye*)

Because I Forgot to Wake Up the Cow (Page 42)
STRUCTURES
- Simple past regular verbs: *miss/missed,*
- Simple past irregular verbs: *forget/forgot*
- Verb + infinitive: *forgot to wake up..., forgot to go..., forgot to shut..., forgot to tell...*
- Adverbial Clauses of reason (cause and effect): *Because..., so... Because..., so...*
- Definite article the: *the cow, the cat*
- Prepositional phrases: *to the store*
- Two-word verbs: *wake up*
- Subject pronouns: *I, we*

PRONUNCIATION
- *T* sound of the past ending on *missed*
- Final *ch* sound on *lunch*
- rhyming patterns: *store/door/floor*

VOCABULARY
- Animal names: *cow, cat, dog, bird*
- *Store, door, floor, lunch*

The Backpack Chant (Page 43)
STRUCTURES
- Simple present information question with *what: What's in your backpack?*
- Indefinite article *a: a calculator*
- Possessive adjectives: *your*
- Prepositional phrases: *in your backpack, on a ring*

PRONUNCIATION
- *Z* sound of the plural *s: things, pens, candy bars, scissors, pencils*
- *S* sound of the plural *s: textbooks, notebooks, paperclips, thumbtacks*
- Contractions: *What's*
- Rhyming patterns: *thing/ring/string/everything*

VOCABULARY
- Classroom objects: *backpack, textbooks, notebooks, paperclips, thumbtacks, pens, pencils, calculator, scissors, string*
- Expressions: *Lots of* (many)

Teacher's Notes New Chants

Early Bird (Page 44)

STRUCTURES
- Simple present affirmative statements: *I'm an early bird., She loves to get up..., I'm a night owl.*
- Indefinite articles *a/an: an early bird, a night owl*
- Definite article *the: the sun, the moon*
- Prepositional phrases: *in the morning, at night*
- Subject Pronouns: *I, she, he*
- Quantifier + adjective: *very early*
- Two-word verbs: *get up*
- Verb + Infinitive: *I love to get up..., I hate to get up...*

PRONUNCIATION
- Contractions: *I'm, she's, he's*
- Reduction of *to* to *t': I love to get up., She loves to get up., I hate to get up., He hates to get up.*

VOCABULARY
- Expressions: *early bird* (a person who gets up early), *night owl* (a person who stays up late)
- *Morning, night, early, late, sun, moon*

The Homework Chant (Page 45)

STRUCTURES
- Simple present affirmative statements: *Mary does homework., Mary loves homework.*
- Question in statement structure (to indicate surprise or call for confirmation): *Mary loves homework?, Harry hates homework?*
- Short confirmation: *That's right!*

PRONUNCIATION
- Rising question intonation on *Mary loves homework?, Harry hates homework?*
- Contractions: *That's*

VOCABULARY
- Expressions for time: *early in the morning, late at night*
- Exclamations: *That's right!* (emphatic "yes")

The Broccoli Chant (Page 46)

STRUCTURES
- Simple present affirmative statements: *I hate broccoli., I love broccoli., I'm crazy about it., I hope we have it for lunch today.*
- Simple present negative statements: *I really don't like it., I don't know why., I can't stand it., I hope we don't have it for lunch today!*
- Short affirmative response: *So do I.*
- Simple present information questions with *What: What can I say?*

PRONUNCIATION
- Reduction of *can* to *c'n: What can I say?*
- Reduction of *today* to *t'day: I hope we have it for lunch today.*
- Contractions: *I'm, don't, can't*
- Rhyming patterns: *I/why, say/today*

VOCABULARY
- *Hate, love, like, say, have, know, lunch, today*
- Expressions: *I don't know why. I can't stand it.* (strong negative dislike), *I'm crazy about it.* (strong positive statement for liking something)

The Sad Dog Song (Page 48)

STRUCTURES
- Simple present affirmative statements: *I want to be a C-A-T., I want to be a cat, like that one. He wants to be a cat., He wants to be a cat like I am.*
- Simple present negative statements: *I don't want to be a D-O-G. He doesn't want to be a D-O-G.*
- Simple present information questions with *What: What's the matter?*
- Definite article *a: a dog, a cat*
- Indefinite article *the: What's the matter?*
- Commands: *Don't feel bad, ...tell me, please., Listen to my sad dog song.*
- Modal *can* for ability: *What can I do?*

PRONUNCIATION
- *S* sound of the third person *s: He wants to be a D-O-G.*
- Contractions: *what's, don't, doesn't*
- The names of the letters of the alphabet: *D,O,G,C,A,T*
- Rhyming patterns: *sad/bad, do/blue, wrong/song*

VOCABULARY
- Animal names: *dog, cat*
- *Sad, blue, good, problem, song, one*
- Expressions: *What's the matter?* (What's wrong?)

The Four Seasons Song (Page 50)

STRUCTURES
- Commands: *Girls stand up and sing., Boys stand up and sing., Everybody sing.*
- Two-word verbs: *stand up, turn into*

PRONUNCIATION
- *Z* sound of the third person *s: Spring turns into summer.*
- *Z* sound of the plural *s: girls, boys*

VOCABULARY
- Seasons: *autumn, winter, spring, summer*
- *Boys, girls, everybody, stand up, turn into*

The Happy Kangaroo Song (Page 51)

STRUCTURES
- Simple present affirmative statements: *I'm a happy kangaroo., I'm happy, too.*
- Simple present information questions with *How: How are you?*
- Subject pronouns: *I, you*
- Indefinite article *a: I'm a happy kangaroo.*

PRONUNCIATION
- Contractions: *I'm*
- Rhyming patterns: *you/kangaroo/too*

VOCABULARY
- Expressions: *How are you?* (greeting)
- *Happy, kangaroo*

Where's Diana (Page 52)

STRUCTURES
- Simple present affirmative statements: *I want to see Diana every day.*
- Simple present information questions with *Where: Where's Diana?, Where is she?, Where's Roberto?*
- Verb + infinitive: *I want to see...*

PRONUNCIATION
- Contractions: *Where's*
- Reduction of *want to* to *wanna: I want to see Diana every day.*
- The names of the letters of the alphabet: *D,I,A,N,A, R,O,B,E,R,T,O*

VOCABULARY
- Time Expressions: *every day*

Teacher's Notes New Songs

Giraffes Drink Water (Page 53)

STRUCTURES
- Simple present affirmative statements: *Giraffes drink water., Giraffes eat leaves.,*
- Simple present negative statements: *They don't like beetles., Giraffes hate bees.*
- Adverbial clauses with *when: When they're very hungry, giraffes eat trees!*

PRONUNCIATION
- *S* sound of the plural: *giraffes*
- *Z* sound of the plural: *beetles, bees, trees*
- *Contractions: don't, they're*
- *Ch* sound in *cheese*
- Rhyming patterns: *leaves/cheese/ bees/trees*

VOCABULARY
- Animal names: *giraffes, beetles, bees*
- *Cheese, water, leaves, trees, drink, eat, like, hate, almost never*

The Toothbrush Song (Page 54)

STRUCTURES
- Commands: *Brush your teeth with a toothbrush., Comb your hair with a comb., Brush your hair..., Wash your face..., Dry your face...*
- Possessive adjectives: *your*

PRONUNCIATION
- *Sh* sound in *toothbrush, hairbrush*
- Final *th* sound in *washcloth, teeth, with*

VOCABULARY
- *Toothbrush, hairbrush, washcloth, towel, comb, teeth, hair, face, brush, comb, wash, dry*

T—Telephone (Page 55)

Note: Structures are not listed because this is a vocabulary chant.

PRONUNCIATION
- Sounds of the letters: *T, V, C*

VOCABULARY
- *Telephone, video, TV, cellular, cell phone, Hello*

PERFORMANCE NOTES
- Have students form the letters T and V and C with their hands when performing this chant.
- Have students hold an imaginary mobile phone to their ear and say "Hello" as they chant the words *cell phone, cell phone* at the end of the chant.

He's an Ethiopian (Page 56)

STRUCTURES
- Simple affirmative present statements: *He's an Ethiopian., He's from Ethiopia., Every day he goes to school in Ethiopia., Every night he goes to bed in Ethiopia., Every night he falls asleep in Ethiopia.*
- Two-word verbs: *wake up*
- Subject pronouns: *he*
- Prepositional phrases: *in Ethiopia*
- Indefinite article *an: an Ethiopian*

PRONUNCIATION
- Contractions: *He's*
- *S* sound of the third person *s: He wakes up.*
- *Z* sound of the third person *s: He goes to school..., He goes to bed...., He falls asleep...*

VOCABULARY
- Time expressions: *every morning, every day, every night*
- *Fall asleep, wake up, go to bed, go to school*

Teacher's Notes New Songs

Back in School (Page 58)

STRUCTURES
- Simple present affirmative statements: *Everybody's happy to be back in school., Everybody's happy to be back in the classroom..., All of us are back in school., All of the teachers are back in school.*
- Prepositional phrases: *in school, in the classroom, in the hall, on the school bus*

PRONUNCIATION
- *S* sound of the plural *s: students*
- *Z* sound of the plural *s: teachers*
- Contractions: *everybody's*

VOCABULARY
- School vocabulary: *school, classroom, hall, school bus, teachers, students*
- Time expression: *back again*
- *Everybody, happy*

The Good Student Song (Page 60)

STRUCTURES
- Simple present affirmative statements: *He gets up early and goes to English class..., She comes home early and does her homework.*
- Simple present negative statements: *He's never ever late to school., She's never ever late to school.*
- Subject pronouns: *he, she*
- Possessive adjectives: *his, her*
- Two-word verbs: *get up*
- Irregular third person plural *does: She comes home early and does her homework.*

PRONUNCIATION
- *S* sound of the third person plural *s: He gets up early...*
- *Z* sound of the third person plural *s: She comes home early and does her homework.*
- Contractions: *he's, she's*

VOCABULARY
- Time expressions: *early, late, never ever* (emphatic form)
- *School, homework, English class*

Danny Bought a D-O-G (Page 62)

STRUCTURES
- Simple past affirmative statements: *Danny bought a D-O-G., Danny lost his D-O-G., Danny found his D-O-G.*
- Irregular past verbs: *buy/bought, lose/lost, find/found*
- Indefinite article *a: a dog*
- Possessive adjectives: *his*

PRONUNCIATION
- Reduction of the *h* sound in *his: lost his D-O-G, found his D-O-G*
- Reduction of the final *t* sound in bought: *Danny bought a D-O-G.*

VOCABULARY;
- *Dog, bought, lost, found*
- Expressions: *Oh gee* (to express pleasure/sympathy)

Hi, How Are You? (Page 64)

STRUCTURES
- Simple present affirmative statements: *I'm fine, thank you.*
- Simple present information questions with *how: How are you?*

PRONUNCIATION
- Contractions: *I'm*

VOCABULARY
- Greeting: *Hi, How are you?*
- Response: *I'm fine, thank you.*

Teacher's Notes New Songs

The Happy Weekend Song (Page 65)

Note: Structures are not listed because this is a vocabulary song. It teaches the days of the week.

VOCABULARY
- Days of the week: *Monday, Tuesday, Wednesday, Thursday, Friday, Saturday, Sunday*

PERFORMANCE NOTES
- Have students form a circle and very slowly walk in one direction pretending they are very, very tired and bored as they sing *Monday, Tuesday, Wednesday, Thursday.*
- Have students change direction and continue singing the same four days very, very slowly.
- Have students suddenly jump around, full of joy, as they then quickly sing *Friday, Saturday, Sunday.* Then they shout out "Happy Weekend!"

I Bought a House for My Pig (Page 66)

STRUCTURES
- Simple past affirmative statements: *I bought a house for my pig., I put my pig on the floor., I bought a house for my cat., I put my cat on the floor*
- Irregular past verbs: *buy/bought, put/put, feed/fed, get/got, can't/couldn't*
- Simple past negative statements: *...he couldn't get out of the door.*
- Comparative adjectives: *bigger*
- Commands: *Look at him now!, Look at her now!*
- Prepositional phrases: *on the floor, out of the door*
- Subject pronouns: *I*
- Object pronouns: *him, her*
- Possessive adjectives: *my*
- Indefinite article *a: a house*
- Intensifier: *so*

PRONUNCIATION
- Rhyming patterns: *pig/big, floor/door, wow/now, cat/fat*

VOCABULARY
- *Pig, cat, house, floor, big, door, now*
- Expressions: *Wow!* (to express amazement or great pleasure)

If It Rains (Page 68)

STRUCTURES
- Conditional affirmative statements: *If it rains, I'll wear my raincoat.*
- Conditional negative statements: *If it doesn't rain, I won't.*
- Adverbial clauses with *when: When it's cold, I always wear my gloves., When it isn't cold I don't.*
- Subject pronouns: *I, we*
- Possessive adjectives: *my, our*

PRONUNCIATION
- Contractions: *I'll, we'll, doesn't, don't, won't, isn't*
- *Z* sound of he third person *s: rains, snows, comes*
- *Z* sound of the plural *s: gloves, sandals*
- initial *ch* sound in *chill*
- Rhyming patterns: *won't/don't, will/chill*

VOCABULARY
- Clothing vocabulary: *raincoat, gloves, coat, sandals*
- *Chill, cold, sun, rain, snow*
- Expressions: *brand new* (very new)